Top 10 Stress Management Techniques for Entrepreneurs

RJC Creatrix Publishing

CONTENTS

Introduction 5

Top 10 Stress Management Techniques 6

Technique 1: Stress Management through
Meditation 7

Technique 2: Stress Management through
Prayer 10

Technique 3: Stress Management through Self
Belief 12

Technique 4: Stress Management through
Positive Self Affirmations 14

Technique 5: Stress Management through Time
Management 15

Technique 6: Stress Management through
Delegation of Tasks 17

Technique 7: Stress Management through
Organizing Life 18

Technique 8: Stress Management through Having Intimate Relationships 19

Technique 9: Stress Management through Practicing Peaceful Living................................ 20

Technique 10: Stress Management through Constant Renewal, Rest and Relaxation.......... 23

Introduction

Stress is a situation where life's demands on a person exceed that person's ability to cope up with the situation. Every human being has the ability to recognise stress and the innate intelligence to respond with. Often a person under stress is wired to have either 'fight' or 'flight' response.

Stress is an outside stimulus which, most often, adversely affects our physical and psychological temperament. That is, stress affects a person both physically and psychologically.

Stress may be positive or negative. Some stress is good and may have a positive effect. This positive stress is called eustress. However there is a limit to such stress. When a stress begins to affect a person adversely, it is called a negative stress or distress. Positive stress acts as performance motivator and under its pressure a person often performs beyond the threshold limit of his or her capabilities.

Negative stress always results in physical and psychological sufferings. Psychological symptoms of stress include worry, anxiety, depression, hypertension, irritability, insomnia and lack of appetite. Some of the physical conditions under stress are allergies, asthma, heart attack, high blood pressure, overactive thyroid gland, peptic ulcers, gaining weight, lethargy, and swollen eye bags.

Top 10 Stress Management Techniques

1. Practicing Meditation: Simple form of meditation requires deep breathing. Deep breathing is one of the best instant stress relieving techniques
2. Practicing Prayer: Prayer helps a person to have a positive outlook towards life
3. Practicing Self Belief: Everything is possible for a person who believes in himself or herself
4. Self Affirmation Technique: Affirming positive thoughts is one of the best ways to have a positive approach towards life
5. Time Management: Time is the best resource every person possesses. Managing time effectively reduces stress up to a great extent
6. Delegation of Tasks: Delegating some tasks to trustworthy people leaves a person with enough time to focus on important things
7. Organizing Life: Organizing life around important tasks is another important stress management technique
8. Having Intimate Relationships: Relationship stress is one of the biggest stress and it can be managed effectively by having intimate relationships with those who matter the most
9. Practicing Peaceful Living: Every person has a right to a peaceful life. Living in harmony with people and surroundings is a good technique for stress relief
10. Rest and Relaxation: Sleep is another form of stress relieving technique

Technique 1

Stress Management through Meditation

Meditation is an act of contemplation. It is a technique by which one pays attention to the deeper levels of one's mind. In meditation, we let go of ordinary mental activities of thinking, analyzing, problem-solving and memorizing; instead we focus on higher mind and inner awareness. In meditation we focus on the *inherent peace* that lies within us. Meditation brings the peace within towards the surface.

How to Do a Simple Meditation?

Five important criteria for a successful meditation session are a peaceful meditation environment, a comfortable sitting position, stillness of the body, deep breathing and quietness of the mind.

1. Peaceful meditation environment: Choose a peaceful, quiet space

2. Comfortable sitting position

   a. Sit on the floor in a simple cross-legged position. Care should be given that the spine is aligned straight with the body while sitting

   b. If sitting on the floor is difficult, the practitioner may sit on a cushion or a thick folded blanket for more comfortable sitting. Placing a cushion or thick padding under buttocks will also help in the correct alignment of the spine

   c. If sitting cross-legged is difficult, the practitioner may sit comfortably in any of the relaxed sitting positions. However, simple cross-legged position is better

   d. Never sit in a curved position

3. Stillness of the body

   a. Keep the head, neck and trunk of the body aligned straight

   b. Close the eyes and the mouth

   c. Let all facial muscles relax

   d. Relax shoulders and arms

   e. Allow arms and palms rest on the knees

4. Deep serene breathing process

   a. Become aware of your breathing process – inhaling (IN) and exhaling (OUT)

   b. Notice whether the breathing process is shallow or deep (if you are doing shallow breathing that means you are not yet ready for correct breathing meditation. So you have to correct it through conscious efforts of deep breathing. Practicing deep breathing regularly makes your breathing process healthy.)

   c. Do deep breathing (abdominal breathing i.e. breathing diaphragmatically) in a rhythmic manner and count 'in' and 'out' several times until the mind becomes quiet. Breath awareness quiets the mind.

5. Quietness of the mind

   a. Allow the mind to become quiet and focused

   b. Focus on 'awareness within' for 15 minutes during initial periods of meditation. Meditation duration may be extended to 30 minutes to 1 hour depending on the progress of the practitioner on the path of meditation

Other points to remember

- ✓ Breathing awareness in important to have a successful meditation session

- ✓ Practice meditation with the same sitting position and in the same environment for better results

- ✓ It is not recommended to meditate while lying down as lying posture is not suitable for inducing mental alertness

- ✓ Meditation may do for a few minutes to hours depending on the capacity of the person

Technique 2

Stress Management through Prayer

Every prayer generates immense healing energy in mind, body and soul. Prayer is the most powerful technique to bring about mental, physical and spiritual healing. Prayer is the process of getting into an intimate feeling of connection with the Creator. Prayer can be a way of affirming our rightful desires. Prayer can be a source of drawing strength from an 'invisible source of power'. Our gratitude and thanksgivings may become our prayers.

Healing energy of prayer rejuvenates a person. It fills a person with hope, joy and love. Experiencing the healing energy of prayer at least once a day has its own advantages. Praying for strength indeed increases mental strength. It is always better to start a day with a short thanksgiving prayer. Prayer brings positive changes in all situations. It is said that *a family that prays together stays together.*

Prayer is the art of asking and receiving. The art of asking works in compliance with the universal law of attraction. A prayerful person is a highly energized person who is like strong magnet. Such persons can attract all that they pray for towards their life.

Prayers are positive affirmations of our rightful desires, our dreams, or our life's goals. In prayer we ask for the fulfillment of our rightful desires. For our prayers to be answered, we need ask specifically, and with belief until we get what we want. For the fulfillment of our desires we need to learn to visualize the fulfillment of our desire mentally, and then consciously feel the real manifestation of that desire in our life.

How to Achieve Fulfillment of Desires through Prayers?

1. Take a stock of all your desires

2. Distinguish between right (positive) and wrong (negative) desires based on your value system

3. Eliminate all negative desires

4. Focus on only positive desires. Positive desires are your true desires.

5. Prioritize the desires in order of importance and necessity

6. Focus on the most important true desire now

7. Analyze whether the true desire is in harmony with the growth of your body, mind and spirit

8. During analysis focus on any hindering negative forces that block the realization of this desire

9. Major negative forces that hinders the realization of a true desire are – disbelief, doubts and fears, revenge and resentment, attachment and possessiveness, justification and rationalization, withholding and inability to let go, rejection and disappointment, defiance and resistance, submission, and sacrifice.

10. Try to eliminate all mental blocks by removing all negative forces by using the principles of love and forgiveness.

11. Achieve a mental state of calmness and perfect peace as a peaceful mind generates power for the realization of a desire.

Technique 3

Stress Management through Self Belief

Believe that you can change your stress habit and focus on this intention. Decide that you will never be a 'Ms. /Mr. Hurry Worry'. Never practice stress, not even for a moment; instead practice self-belief. Believe you can, and you will. In due time, your stress habit will vanish completely.

We all believe in the power of thoughts. However, power of belief is stronger than the power of thought. Belief is 'knowing' without analysis and reasoning. Belief just believes without any reasons and proof while a thought is byproduct of 'thinking' and 'reasoning' process. Knowing is more powerful than thinking and reasoning. Knowing is experiencing while a thought has to be put into action in order to experience it.

Power of belief is power of hidden knowledge. Belief is having direct access to the inherent supreme energy latent within us. Power of belief is power of experiencing the invisible. There are two dimensions of our belief - belief in God and self belief.

Self Belief is our knowing that we are created in the image of the Lord Almighty, *the Supreme Power* and therefore we are inherently powerful. The source of our power is our *'spirit'*. Though there is no physical evidence for the presence of 'the spirit' in our body, we are inherently aware of the truth that 'the spirit' dwells within us. This is the faith we have in our 'self'.

Size of Belief Determines Size of Success

Our success is determined by the size of our belief. It is true that the bigger our belief system, the bigger our success in life. Belief emboldens us by removing all our inner fears. Fear is the root cause of every failure. Therefore it is necessary to destroy fear by developing strong belief system.

Belief Requires Action

Belief in God and self belief alone are not sufficient to bring desired results. Remember, the Sacred Law of Cause and Effect; *no action, no results*. Belief which is strengthened by right actions in the right direction in a persistent manner alone produces right results.

There are two groups of people around us. First group of people are full of positive forces, happiness, energy, confidence and faith; we call them charismatic people, people with personal power. They are like magnets. Wherever they go, they attract people and people want to be with them. While second group of people are full of negative forces, fears, complaints, anxieties and doubts. They are so repulsive that nobody wants to be associated with them. When we see the charismatic people with full of attractiveness, vitality and happiness, we secretly wish to be like them. The truth is, every human being has an inherent potential to become a highly magnetic and charismatic person. It is every person's birth right to live a *'fully alive'* life. To be fully alive, we need to do only one thing, *believe in God and believe in Self*. People having personal power are the highly successful people in life.

Technique 4

Stress Management through Positive Self Affirmations

Affirming positive thoughts is a wonderful technique to get rid of your stress habit. Utter silently many times a day that 'I hate my stress habit and I can change this habit'. Speak positive about everything. Never participate in negative speech that induces worries and stress.

Chanting positive affirmations repetitively leaves a person with the feeling of healing and purification. Positive affirmations may be done internally within our mind in silence or by producing the sound audibly.

Other variations of this stress management technique are autosuggestion and self-hypnosis.

Technique 5

Stress Management through Time Management

Stress can be managed effectively through time management. First step in time management is prioritization. Prepare a 'to-do-list' and arrange all things that are to be done in order of its importance. Find time for all important things. Eliminate all unnecessary and least important things from the list.

Time management is about managing our time. Time is the basic resource everyone has got at his or her disposal. Time is often an underestimated yet highly precious resource. It is said that time is money. Still, many of us often waste our precious time without any guilt feeling.

Managing time efficiently, effectively and effortlessly is the key to successful time management. That is, time management is all about effectiveness, efficiency, and effortlessness. Time management is all about taking control of our time.

'Effectiveness' means 'having a definite result within the given time frame'. 'Efficiency' means 'getting desired result with minimum effort'. 'Effortless' means 'getting things done in a natural, easy way without much effort'. The best time manager has all three qualities: effectiveness, efficiency and effortlessness.

Time management is an essential quality required to become an entrepreneur. An entrepreneur is supposed to be effective, efficient and effortless. That is, he or she should be good at time management.

Process of time management has several facets. Major facets of time management are,

1. Preparing action plans and to-do-lists which addresses what must be done?
2. Prioritizing tasks which addresses in what order tasks are to be done?
3. Effective delegation of tasks which addresses how and by who tasks must be completed?
4. Project planning which addresses how much time is required for each task?

Time management allows us to use the available time effectively and efficiently by eliminating unnecessary and unimportant tasks from the list and focusing our energy and time only on important tasks. Time management allows us to plan each day and then each week, and again going forward, months and years effectively and efficiently. Successful time management requires great self discipline.

Time management has three major aspects: planning, monitoring and review process. Total available time is divided for important tasks during planning process and then task progress against the given time is monitored regularly for taking appropriate actions. During review process allotted time is reviewed and adjusted as per the project requirements.

Technique 6

Stress Management through Delegation of Tasks

Find whether you have sufficient time for managing all important things that you have listed in your 'to-do-list'. If not, delegate those tasks where your skills, knowledge and supervision are not required to a trustworthy group. Important personal quality that is required for this is the ability to trust people.

We all need to learn to trust people with important tasks in all areas of our life. When we learn to delegate tasks effectively and efficiently, we are left with enough time for ourselves to organize our life around other important priorities.

Technique 7

Stress Management through Organizing Life

Organizing life around our key life goals eliminates stress from our lives. Determine that your life will be stress-free. Make an action plan towards a 'stress-free' life while keeping equilibrium between professional and personal life. Healthy balance between personal life and career life is the key to stress-free life. Our life can be organized in a better way by following a combination of the practices that are listed below:

1. Set aside a day (Sunday or Monday) for preparing task lists and organizing time
2. Write everything that you plan to do for short term as well as for long term. Prepare an easy and workable 'task list' or 'to do list' for short term goals while prepare an elaborate action plan to plan and execute long term goals
3. Prepare timelines for every important task
4. Never allow procrastination. Just do what you want to do
5. Practice unitasking: Do one thing at a time
6. Allot a place for everything and place everything in its place
7. Simplify life; de-clutter regularly; know when and where to discard unwanted things
8. Do only what is required; have courage to say 'No' to unimportant tasks
9. Take control of your life: Taking charge of your time and resources leads to a stress-free life

Technique 8

Stress Management through Having Intimate Relationships

It is said that relationship stress has the biggest adverse effect on a person's health and well being. Therefore it is important for a person to have loving relationships. Having limited but intimate and loving relationships is an important stress management technique.

Confiding everything to the person we trust is actually the best form of stress management. Actually, spending time with our loved ones takes away all stress from our lives. Being friendly with positive people also brings joy to our life.

Technique 9

Stress Management through Practicing Peaceful Living

Peaceful living is the best remedy for a stressful life. Inner peace eliminates all our stress, worries and anxieties of life. Inner peace allows a person to live in the moment. A peaceful life begins the moment we determine to banish *hurry* and *worry* from our life; the moment we decide that we are not going to be worried about others' opinions and perceptions about us. Everybody has a right to free thinking and free speech. And they think and form opinions based on their perceptions. We cannot change their perceptions. People have a tendency to believe what they perceive. So let us live freely without being bothered about others' opinion about us. Let us live in peace with peaceful ways.

Stress management through practicing peaceful living has four major facets. These are,

1. Stress Management through Living in Harmony with Everyone
2. Stress Management through Good Company
3. Stress Management through Silence and Solitude
4. Stress Management through Spending Time with Nature

Stress Management through Harmony and Cooperation

A peaceful person is marked by lack of violence in speech and action. A peaceful person is blameless and upright in heart. A bright future awaits a man of peace.

Peace is living in harmony with every element of the universe. Peace is cooperation and a peaceful person cooperates with other people for a good cause. A peaceful living is the beginning point of formation of a good society.

A peaceful life begins the moment we determine to banish *hurry* and *worry* from our life; the moment we decide that we are not going to be worried about others' opinions and perceptions about us. Everybody has a right to free thinking and free speech. And they think and form opinions based on their perceptions. We cannot change their perceptions. People have a tendency to believe what they perceive. So let us live freely without being bothered about others' opinion about us. Let us live in peace with peaceful ways.

Peaceful living is the best remedy for a stressful life. Inner peace eliminates all our stress, worries and anxieties of life. Inner peace allows a person to live in the moment.

Stress Management through Good Company

Every human being has a desire to belong to a group of own kind. In order to have a sense of belonging to a group, people live in a society where they feel a sense of belonging and a cultural fit. This is the principle behind formation of clubs, associations and societies.

The level of refinement and civility differs with people. It is always a pleasure to interact with people who are as open-minded as we are; who share same interests that we have. It is a good experience to be in the society of similar-minded people. If one cannot find a good company, it is better off to be alone. The Holy Scriptures say that it is better to be alone than in a bad company.

A bad company always brings negativity to a person through the power of absorption. The Holy Scriptures advise us to form friendships with only good people. As god's children, we all need to strive to be good human beings. A good human being is a carrier of manifested supreme energy. So it always gives us a great pleasure to be in the company of good people.

It is a natural human tendency to focus on the negative more and to absorb it. Sometimes, we end up absorbing too much of negativity from the people around us. If we do not have a vent to release it, we too end up as negative persons with mental blocks, blocked love, peace and joy. A Spanish proverb goes like this, *"live with wolves and you will learn to howl."* Therefore we need to learn to eliminate negative people and toxic relationships from our life.

Stress Management through Silence and Solitude

The Hindu Scriptures mention about *ek tatva nirantar abhyas* (one pointed focus in silence on silence) and extols the virtue of silence as an important path to perfect living. Silence and solitude awakens the creative power within us. Absence of speech and noise creates a peaceful environment and a feeling of isolation. In such an environment it is easy to be left alone with one's own thoughts. In that aloneness one can find solitude, and solitude helps a person to attain an inner silence. In inner silence, a person begins *'self-discovery'*. In stillness of mind a person is able to seek God.

Stress Management through Spending Time with Nature

Spending time with nature is a kind of worship. Being God's children, we are blessed with the most wonderful gift from God - Nature with all its creation. Nature glorifies God's love and peace in each of its elements. That is why, countryside sceneries, wilderness, woods and forests, flora and fauna, flowers, evening clouds, hills and mountains, lakes and rivers, all of these, instil a sense of peace within us. It is our responsibility to guard the treasures of the nature without disturbing its balance.

Technique 10

Stress Management through Constant Renewal, Rest and Relaxation

Negative emotions, boredom with monotonous repetitive daily routine, laziness, negative people and negative circumstances drain a lot of energy from us. Sleep is the best remedy to recharge our 'positive' battery. Meditation, prayer and positive affirmations strengthen our minds. Play and exercise strengthen our body. Getting away to a holiday spot for a few days is also a wonderful form of relaxation.

Sleep as a Stress Management Technique

One of the best stress management techniques that a person can always rely upon is a good sleep. It is said that a human body repairs itself during sleep. Stress hormones released in the blood stream is supposed to be normalized within a short span of time. Otherwise stress-related lifestyle sicknesses become a major life-threatening problem for those who are under constant stress. For adults at least 7- 8 hours of good quality sleep is necessary for getting adequate rest. Quality of sleep is equally important as the number of sleeping hours.